ISBN-10: 1-56647-801-4
ISBN-13: 978-1-56647-801-4

Photography by Bigbamboostock.com

First Printing, December 2006
1 2 3 4 5 6 7 8 9

Mutual Publishing, LLC
1215 Center Street, Suite 210
Honolulu, Hawai'i 96816
Ph: 808-732-1709 / Fax: 808-734-4094
E-mail: info@mutualpublishing.com
www.mutualpublishing.com

Printed in Taiwan

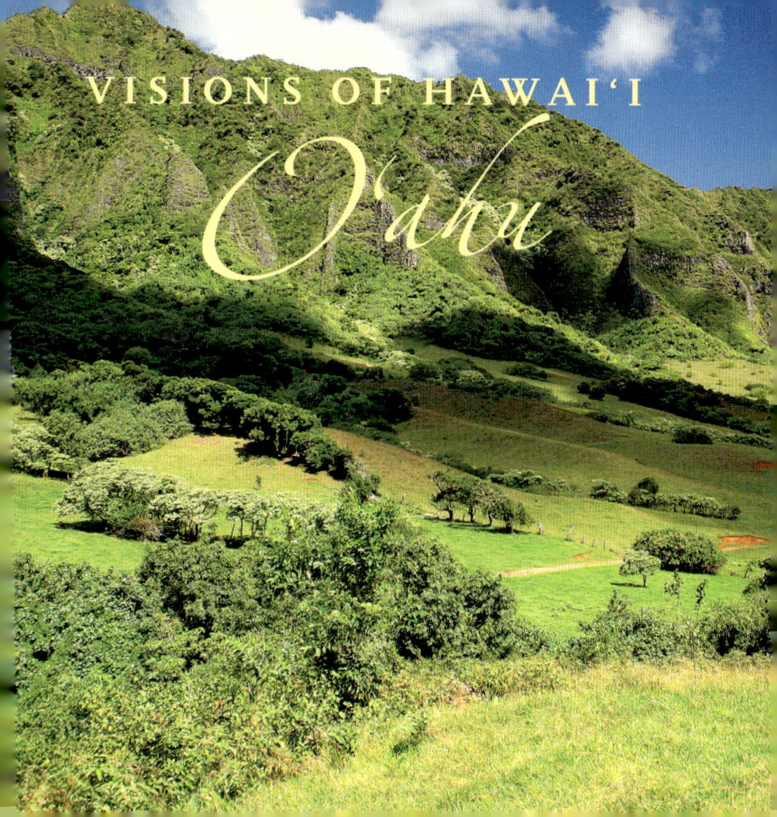
VISIONS OF HAWAI'I
O'ahu

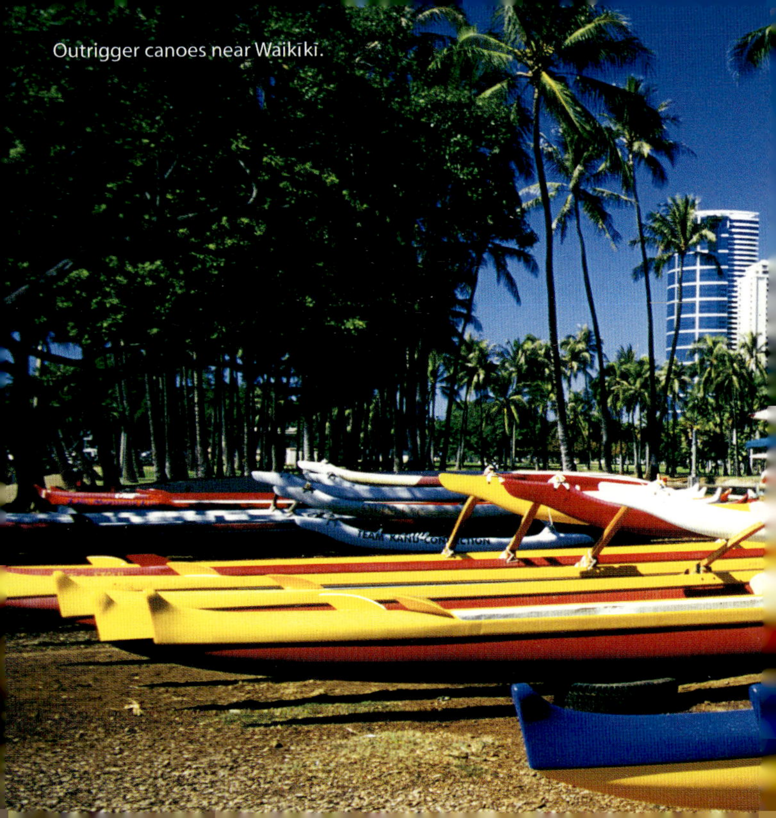

Outrigger canoes near Waikīkī.

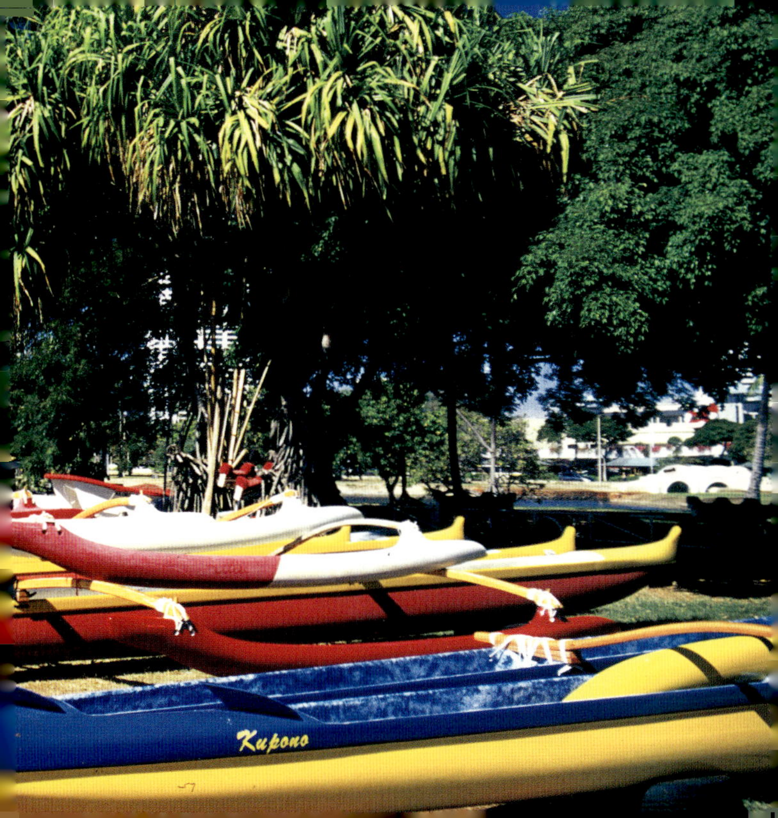
Kupono

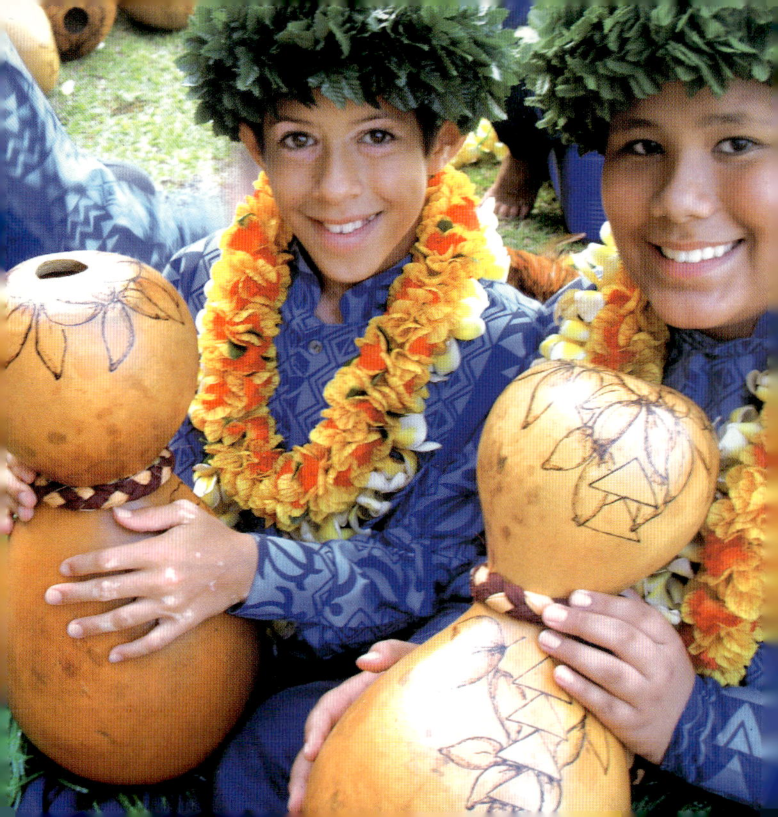

O'ahu

the gathering place

What defines O'ahu? It has the most famous surf in the world, at legendary breaks like Pipeline and Waimea. It has spectacular beaches on every shore: in the south, Waikīkī; the east, Waimānalo; the north, Sunset; the west, Mākaha. It has amazing botanical gardens: Foster and Ho'omaluhia and Lyon Arboretum, all places where an exotic array of

OPPOSITE: Celebrating Kamehameha Day.

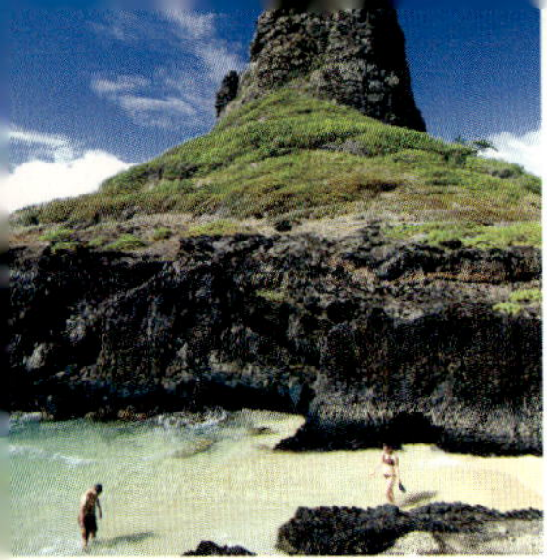

plants thrive in the island's benign climes. It has two mountain ranges, the Wai'anae and the Ko'olau, with cliffs (*pali* in Hawaiian) that drop away precipitously and offer stunning view lines. It has now-extinct volcanic craters: Punchbowl, Koko Head, Diamond Head.

And people—does it have people! Over a million at last count: Hawaiian, Samoan, Chinese, Japanese, Korean, Filipino, Thai, Scottish, Irish, German—you name it. And with the people have come cultures, many of them. Different languages and dialects and accents can be heard on almost every street corner, though pidgin remains the local favorite. *What, boddah*

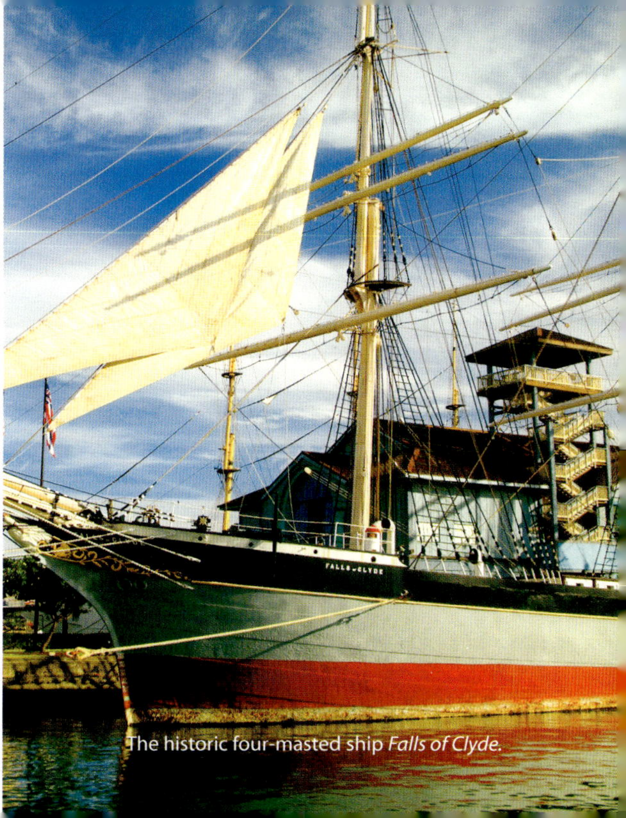

The historic four-masted ship *Falls of Clyde.*

you? O'ahu has learning centers like the Honolulu Academy of Arts and the Bishop Museum and buildings that reflect a variety of architectural styles, from the high rises of Waikīkī to the plantation cottages of Waialua. And let's not forget the food. O'ahu has a huge range of restaurants, everything from sushi bars and Thai takeaways to Mexican cantinas and dim sum haunts. Celebrity chefs have popped up, too—the likes of Sam Choy, Alan Wong, and Roy Yamaguchi—and opened swanky spots that serve a cuisine so sophisticated the whole world knows about it.

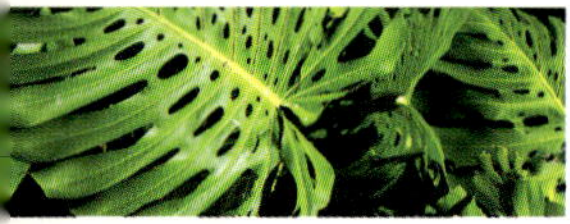

And then there are the two best-loved things about the island: the sunshine and the ocean. They are truly what give us life here in this metropolis in the middle of the sea: the sunshine, which warms our days and keeps us happy; and the ocean, which welcomes us in and invites us to play.

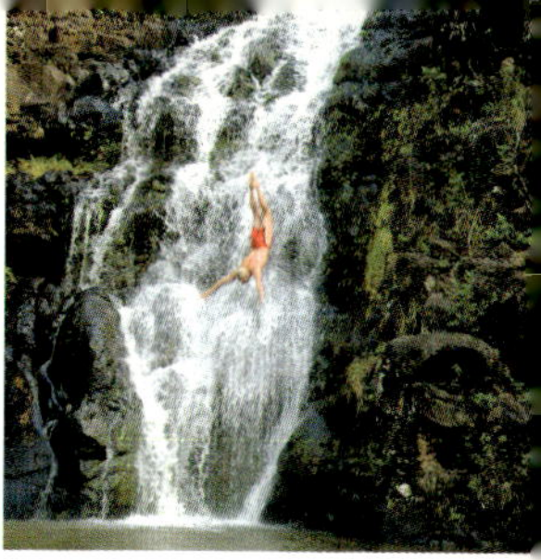

So, back to that question: what defines O'ahu? By now, it should be clear. It's abundance, abundance, abundance.

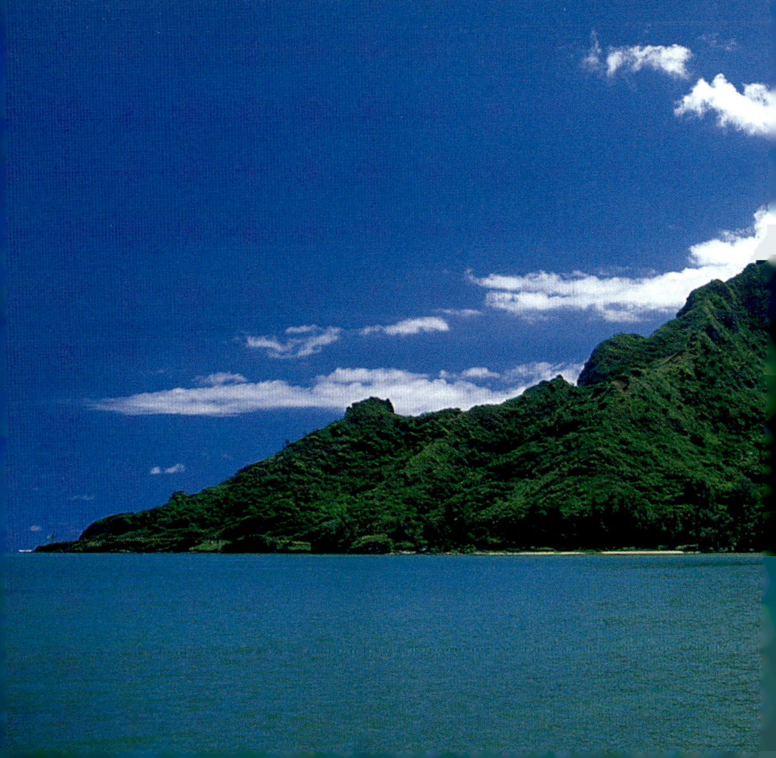

Sailing the waters of Kahana Bay.

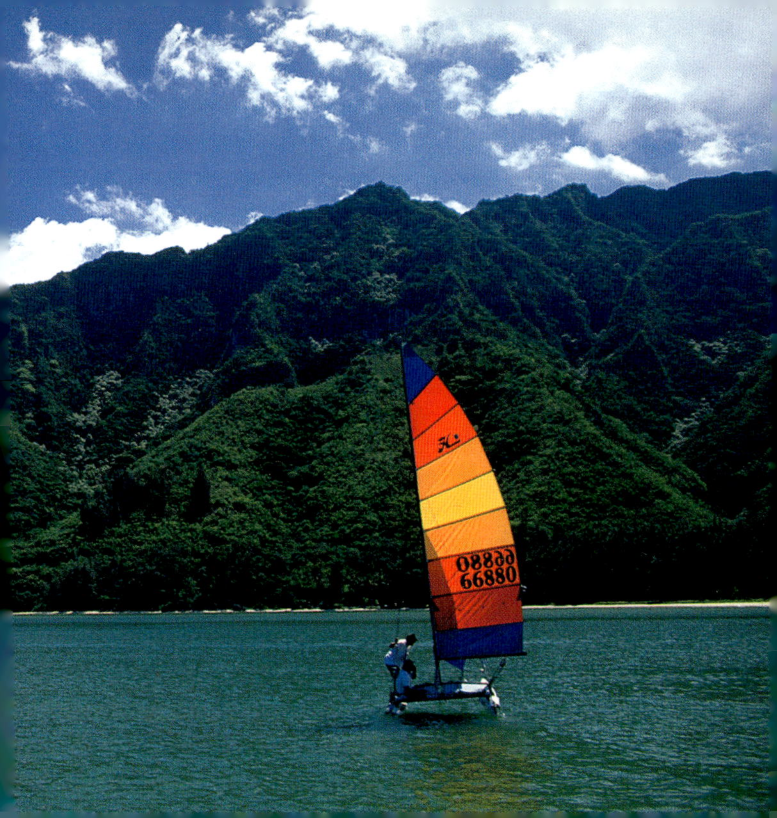
66880

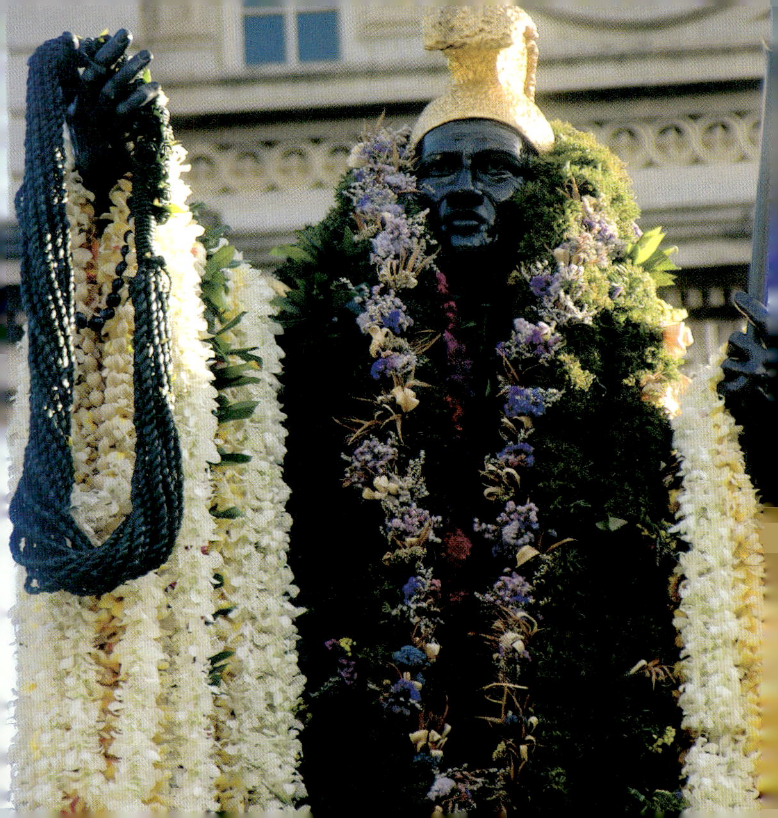

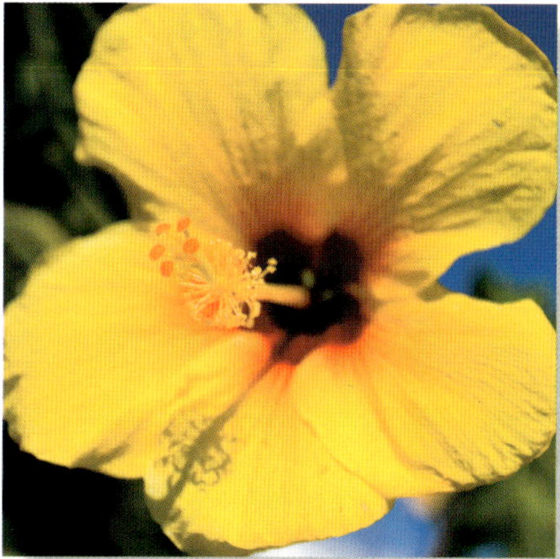

Flowers grace the King Kamehameha statue downtown (left), and almost every backyard on O'ahu.

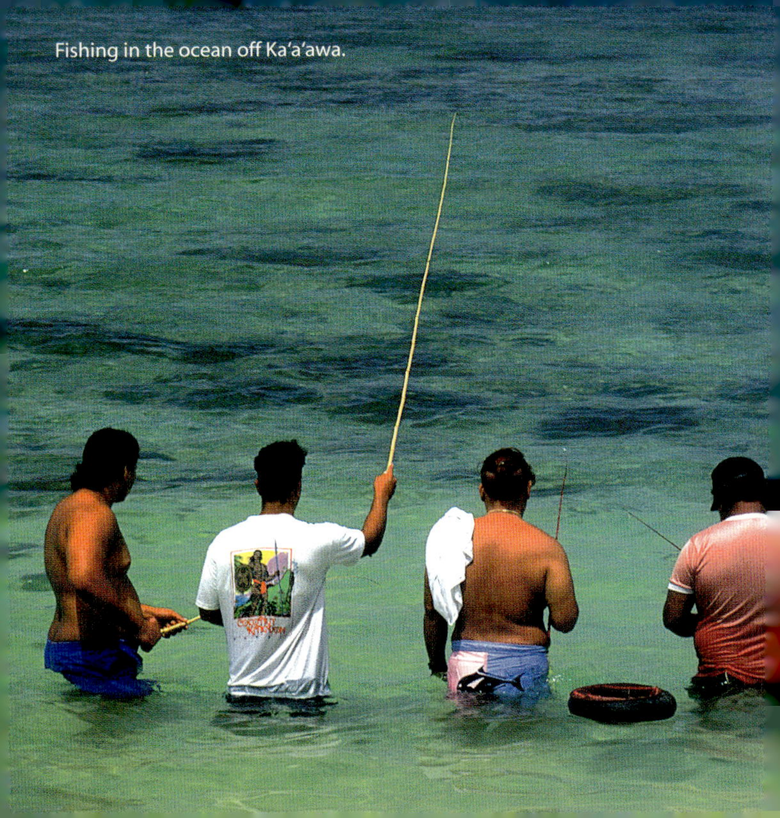

Fishing in the ocean off Ka‘a‘awa.

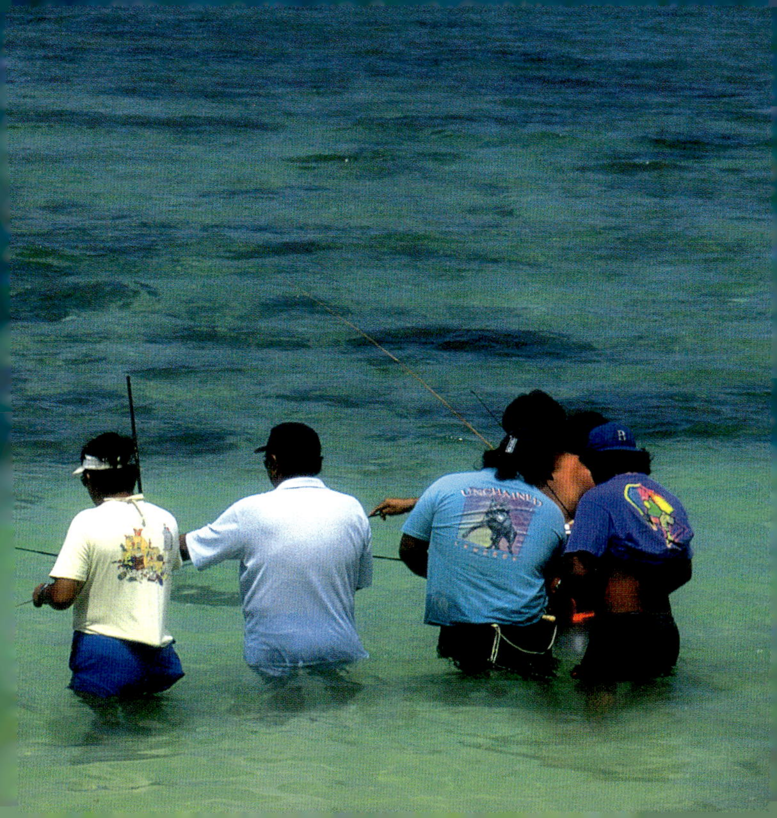
UNCHAINED

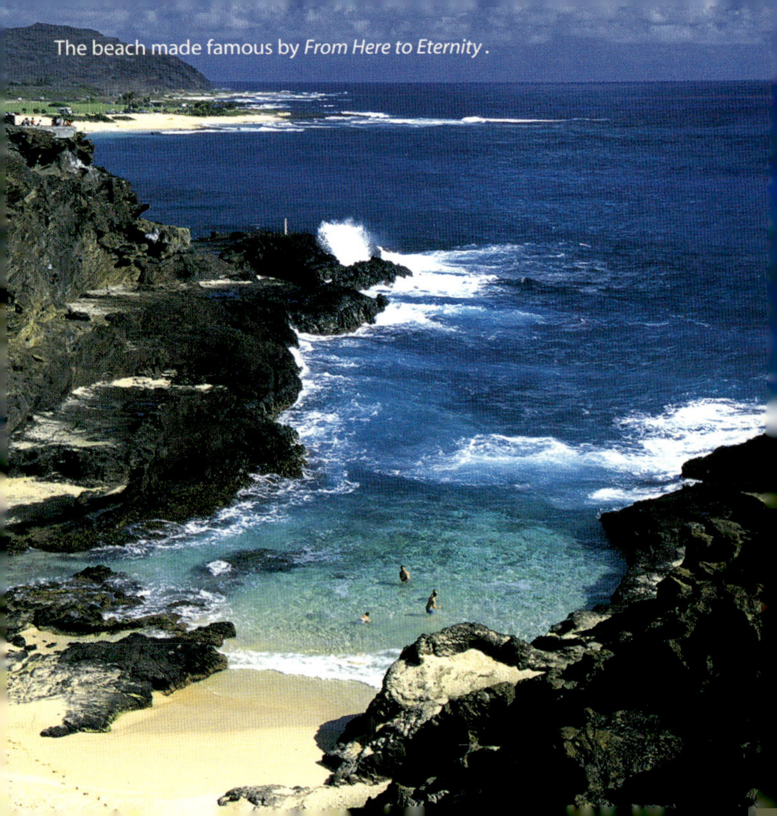

The beach made famous by *From Here to Eternity*.

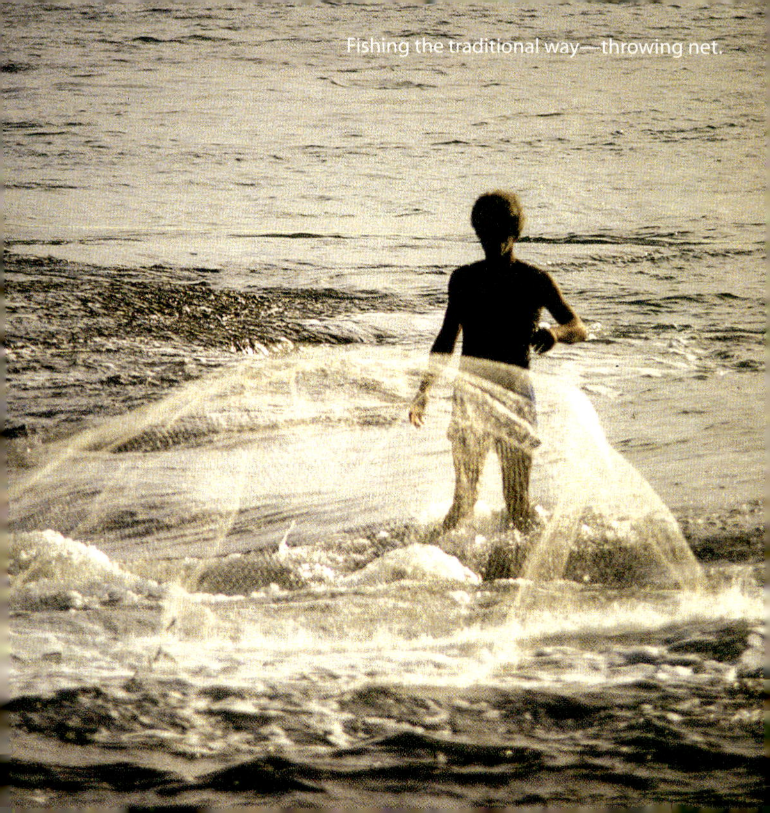

Fishing the traditional way—throwing net.

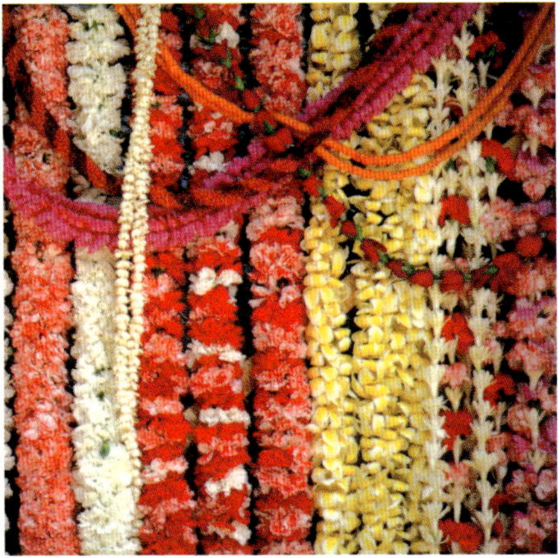

Every day is lei day.

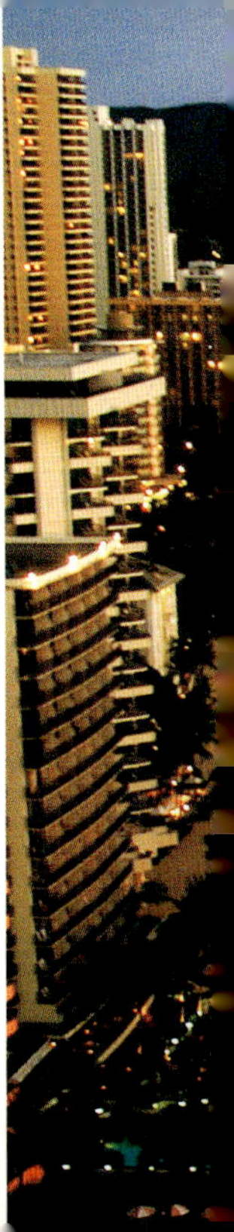

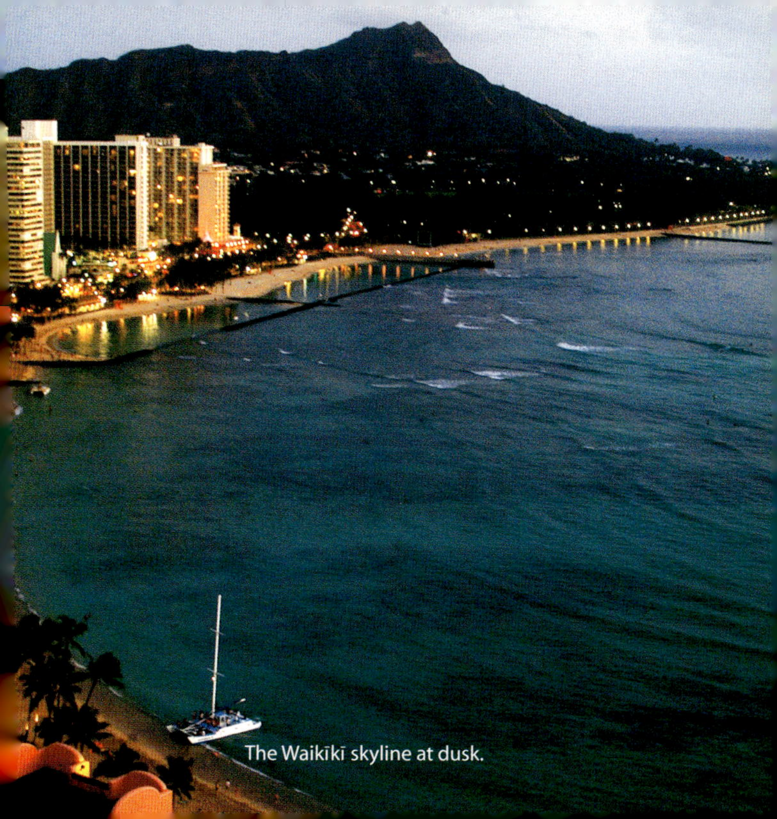

The Waikīkī skyline at dusk.

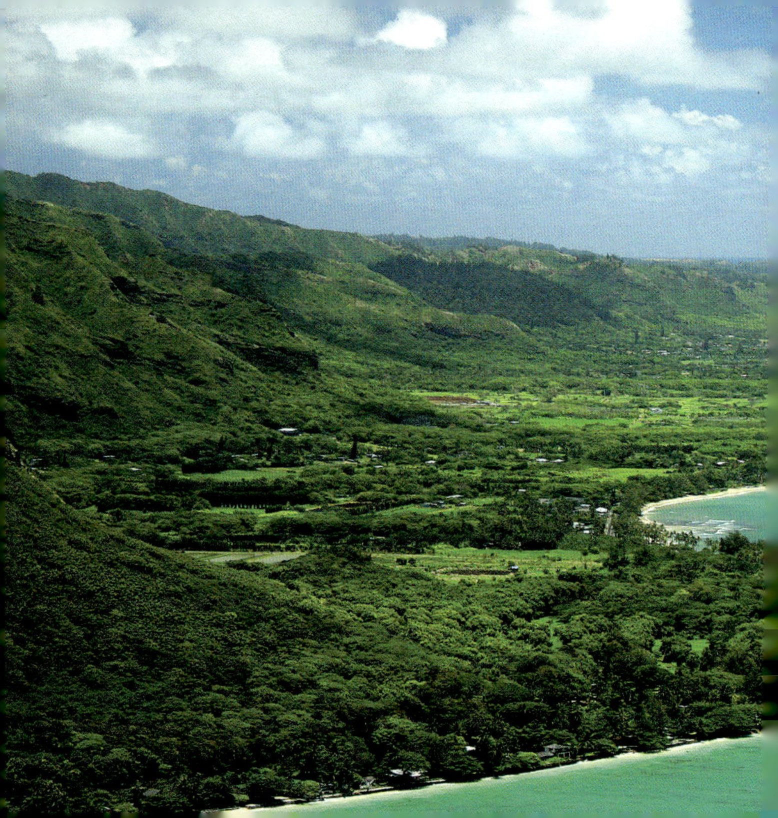

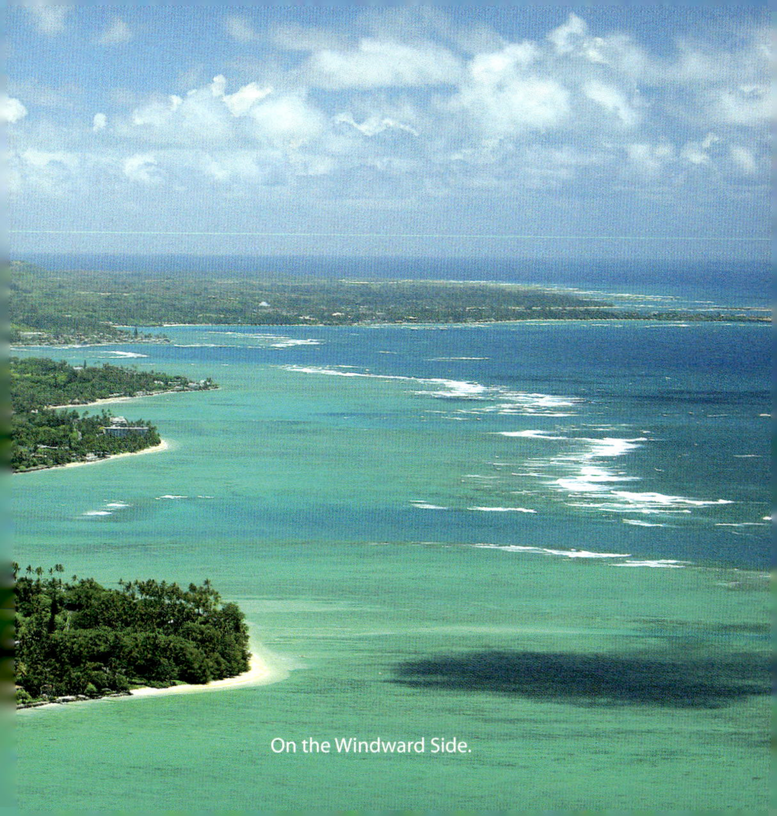

On the Windward Side.

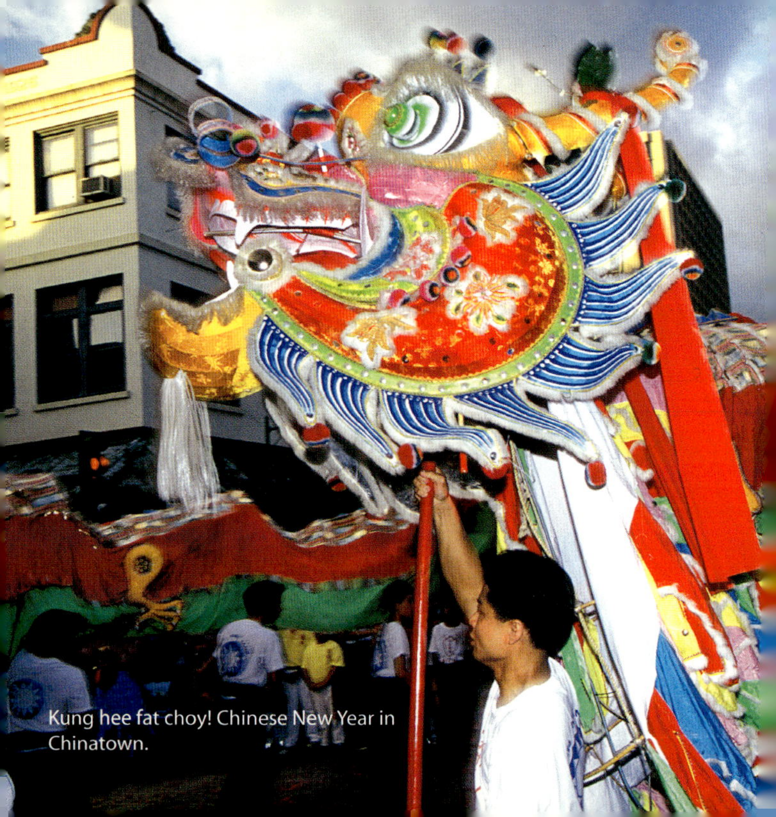

Kung hee fat choy! Chinese New Year in Chinatown.

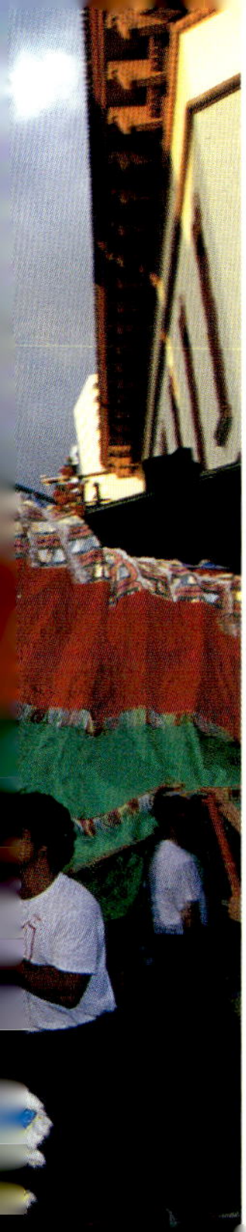

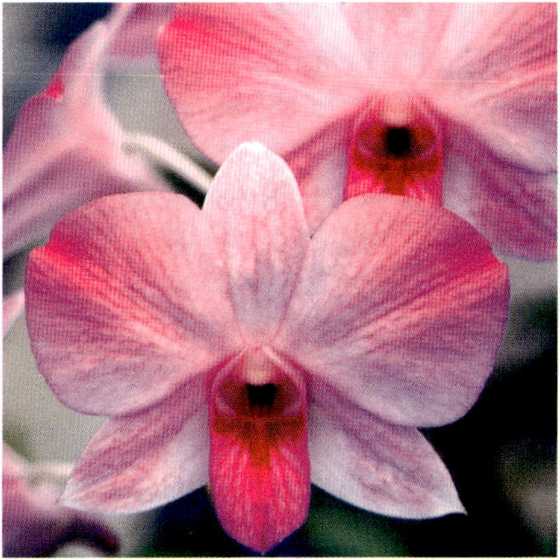

Orchids abound in Honolulu.

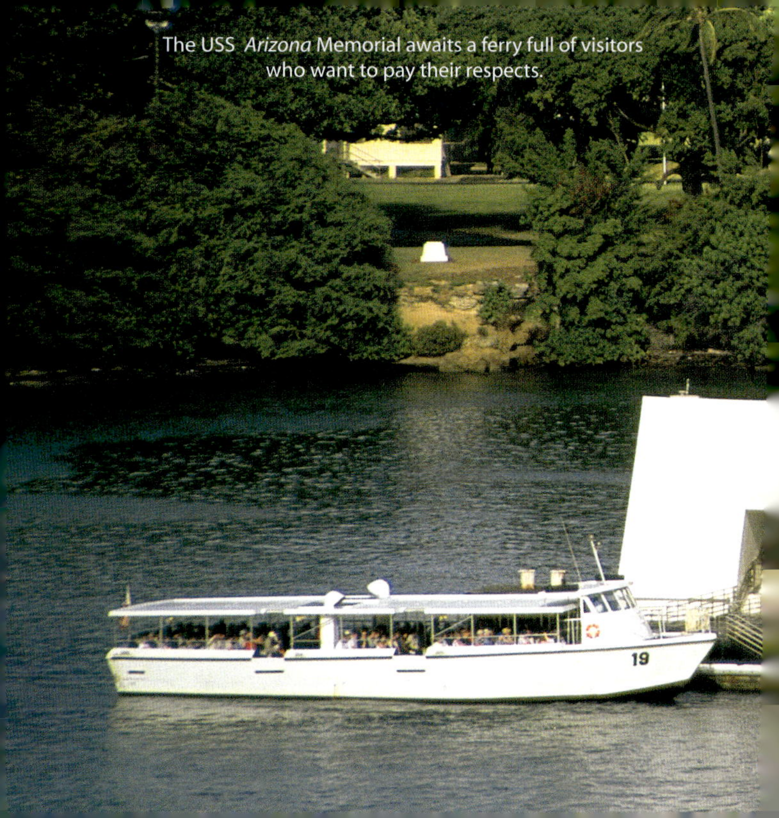

The USS *Arizona* Memorial awaits a ferry full of visitors who want to pay their respects.

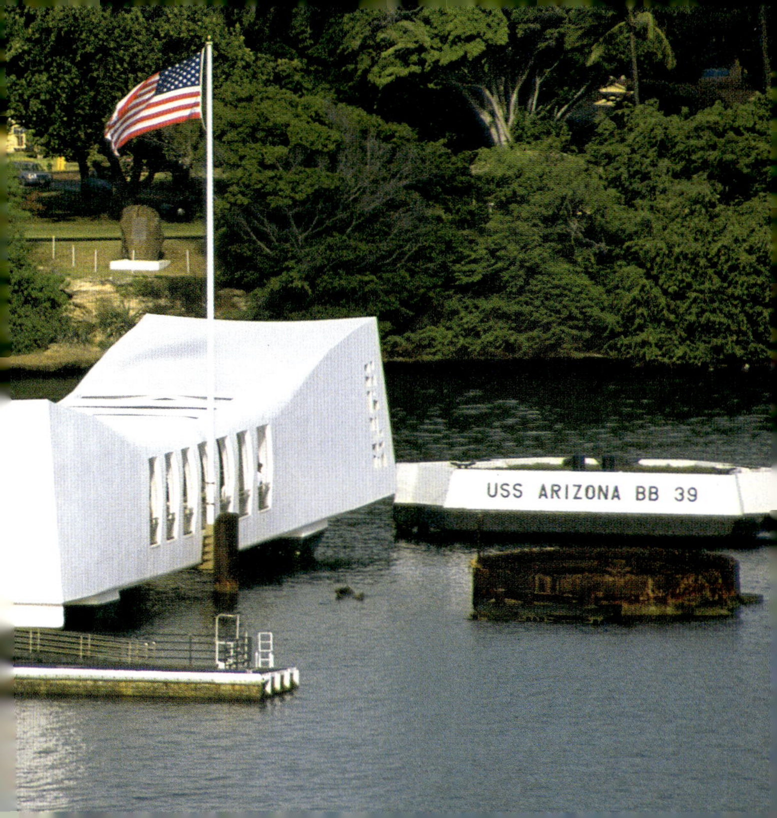
USS ARIZONA BB 39

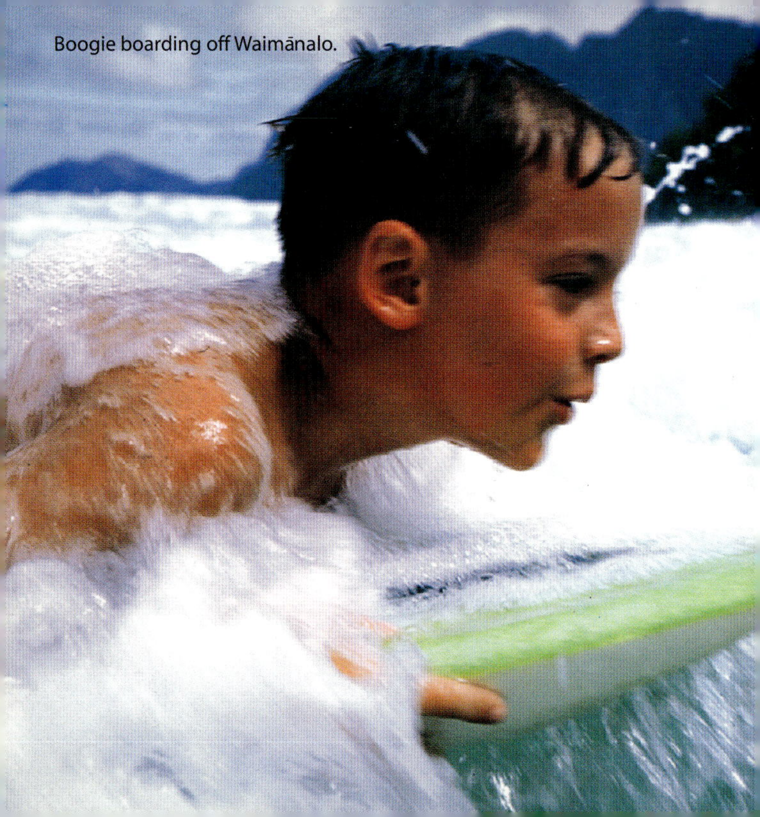
Boogie boarding off Waimānalo.

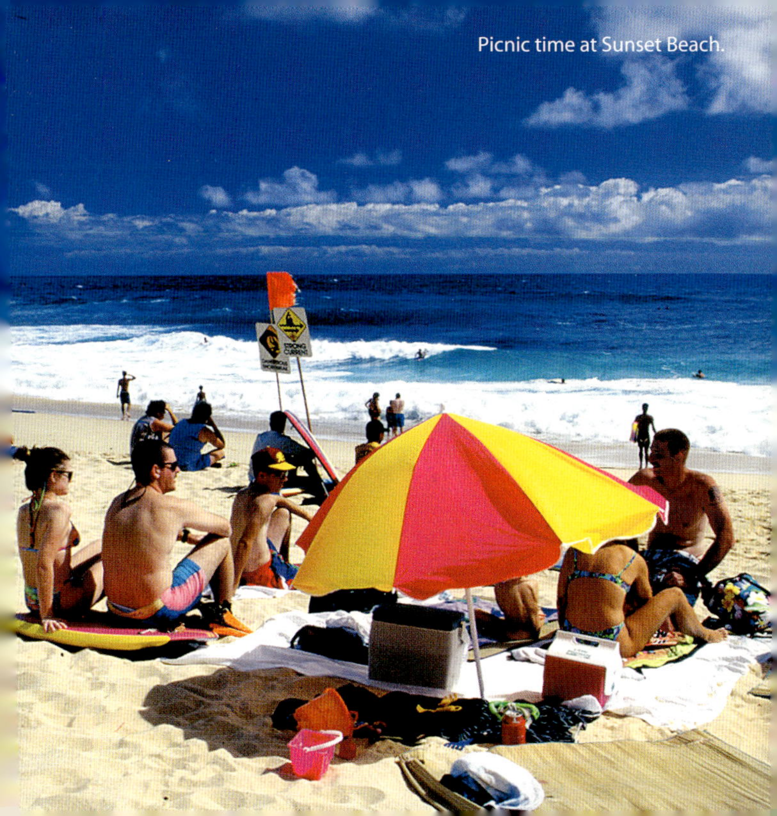

Picnic time at Sunset Beach.

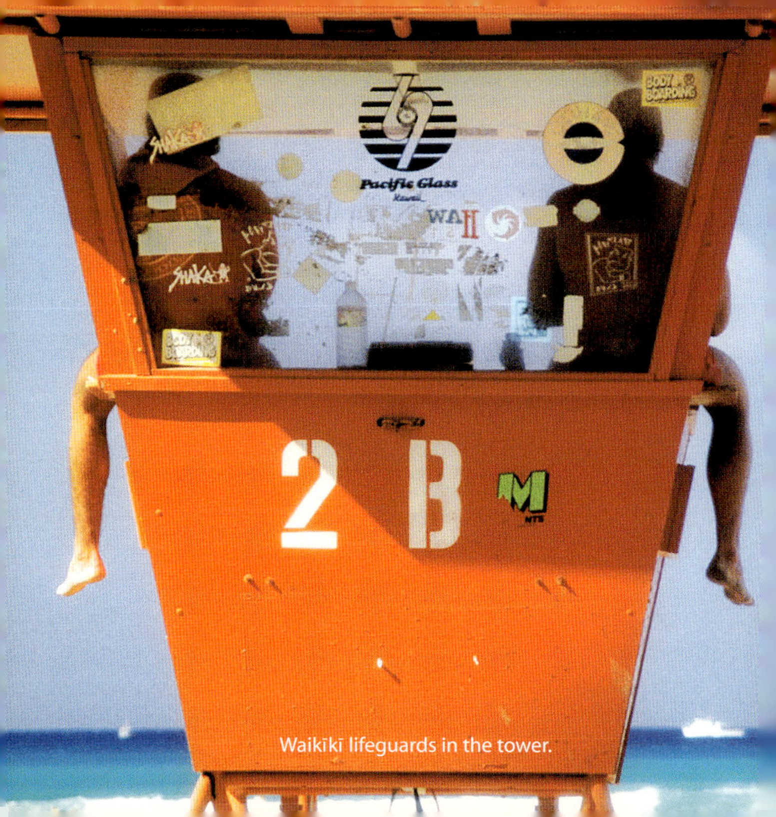

Waikīkī lifeguards in the tower.

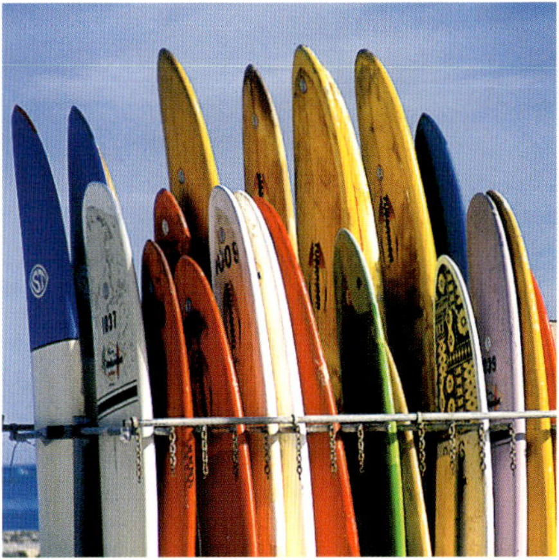

Surfboards for rent.

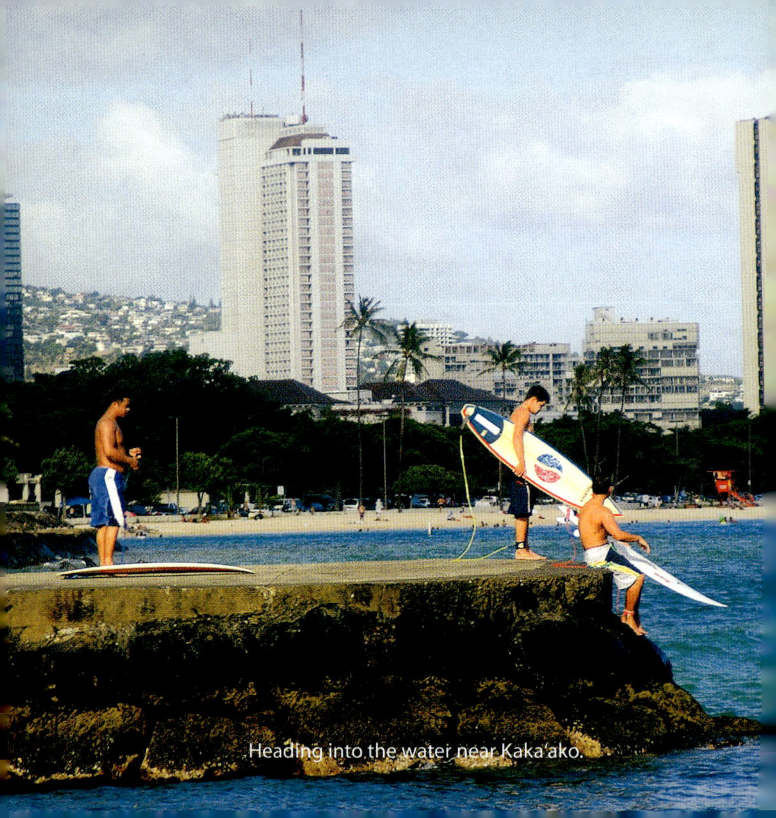

Heading into the water near Kaka'ako.

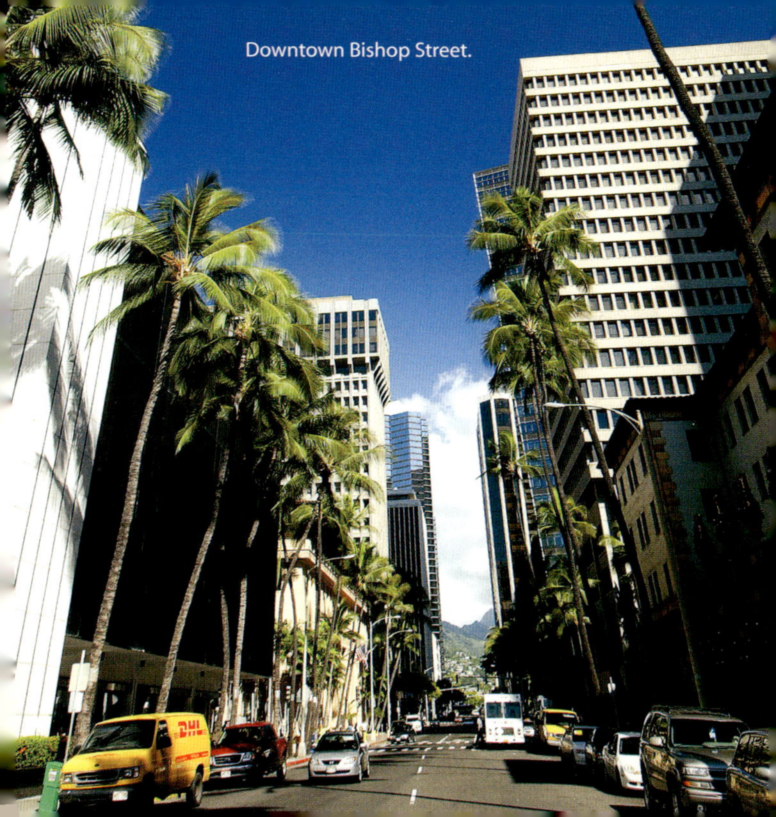

Downtown Bishop Street.

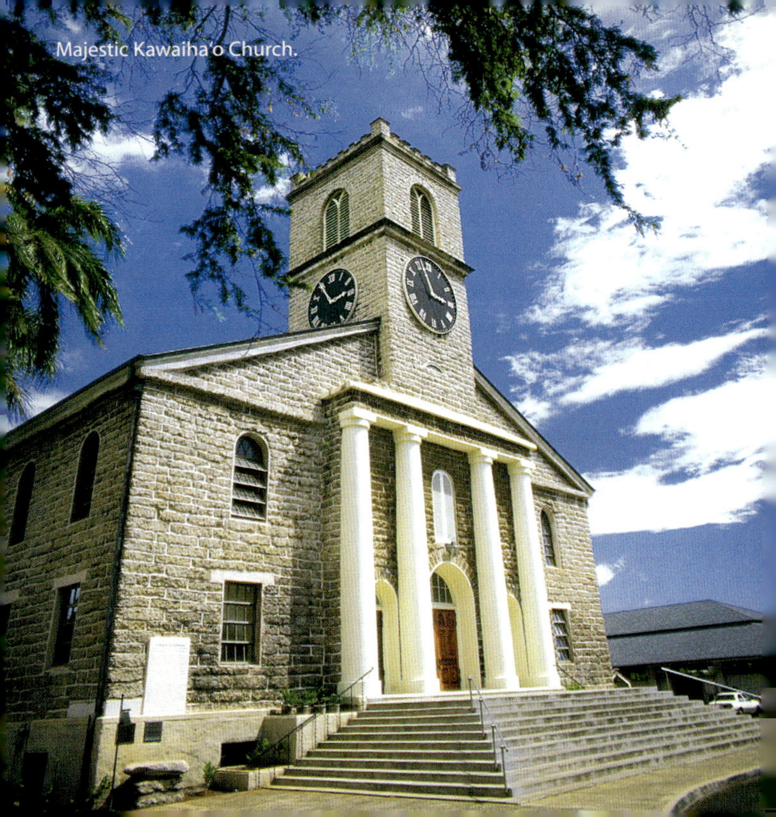

Majestic Kawaiha'o Church.

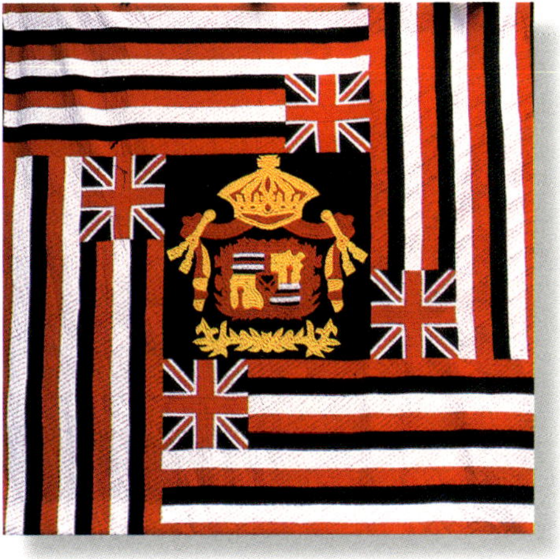

A Hawaiian flags quilt.

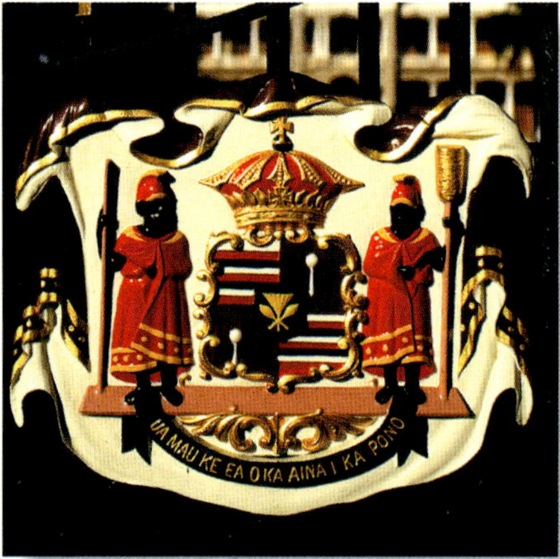

The crest on the ʻIolani Palace gate.

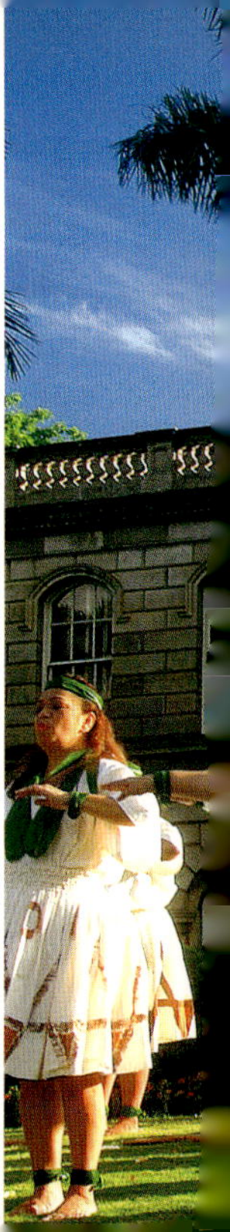

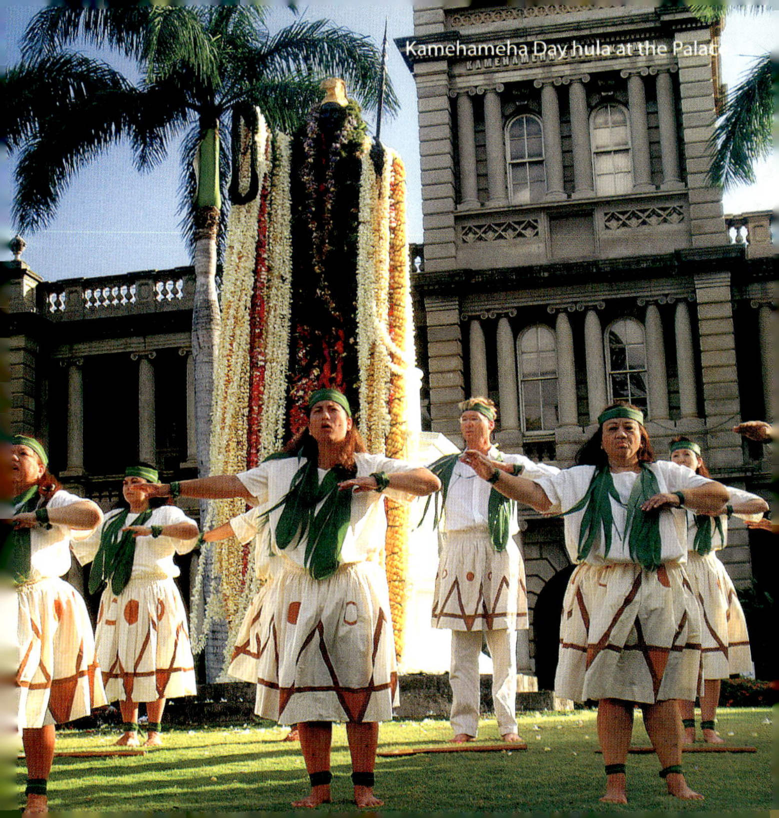

Kamehameha Day hula at the Palace

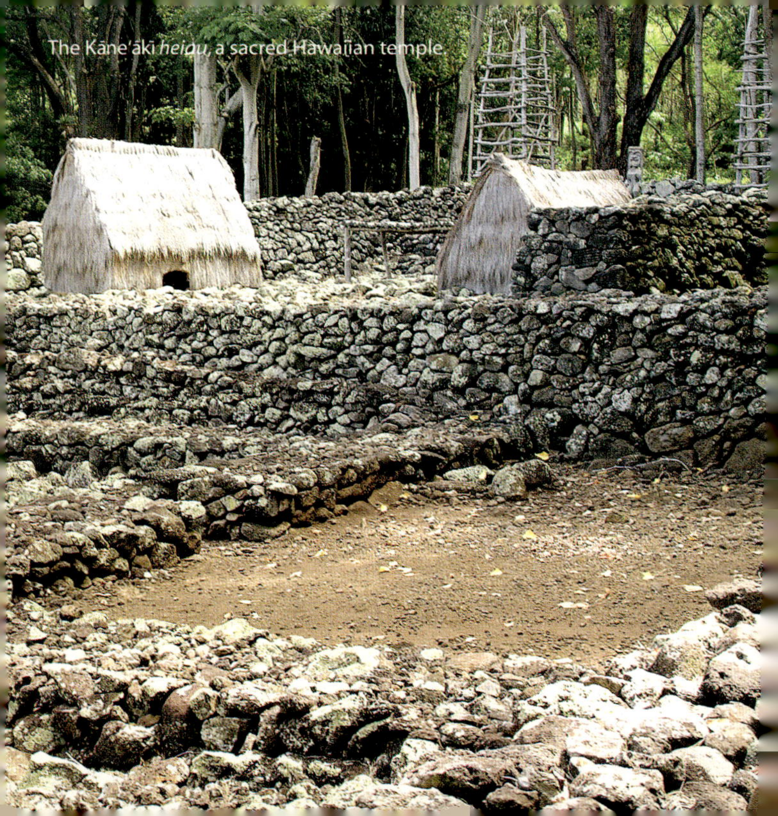

The Kāne'ākī *heiau*, a sacred Hawaiian temple.

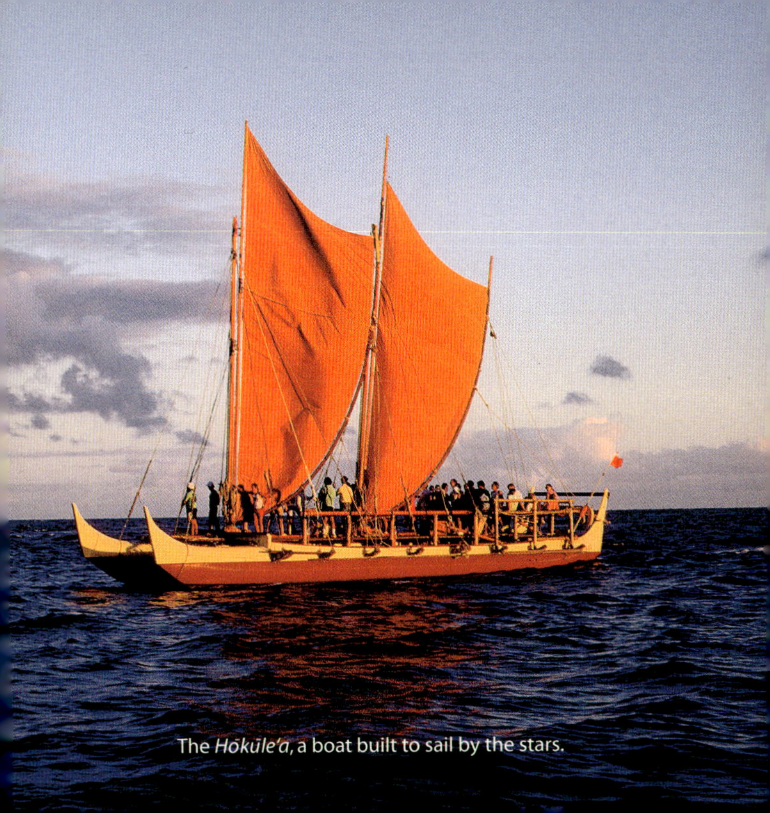

The *Hōkūle'a*, a boat built to sail by the stars.

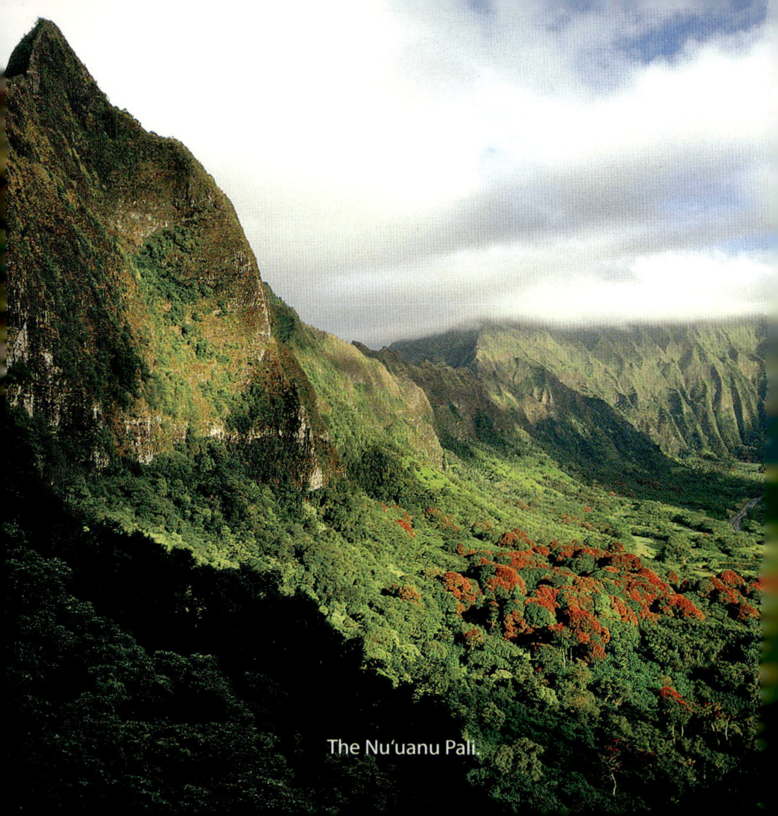

The Nu‘uanu Pali.

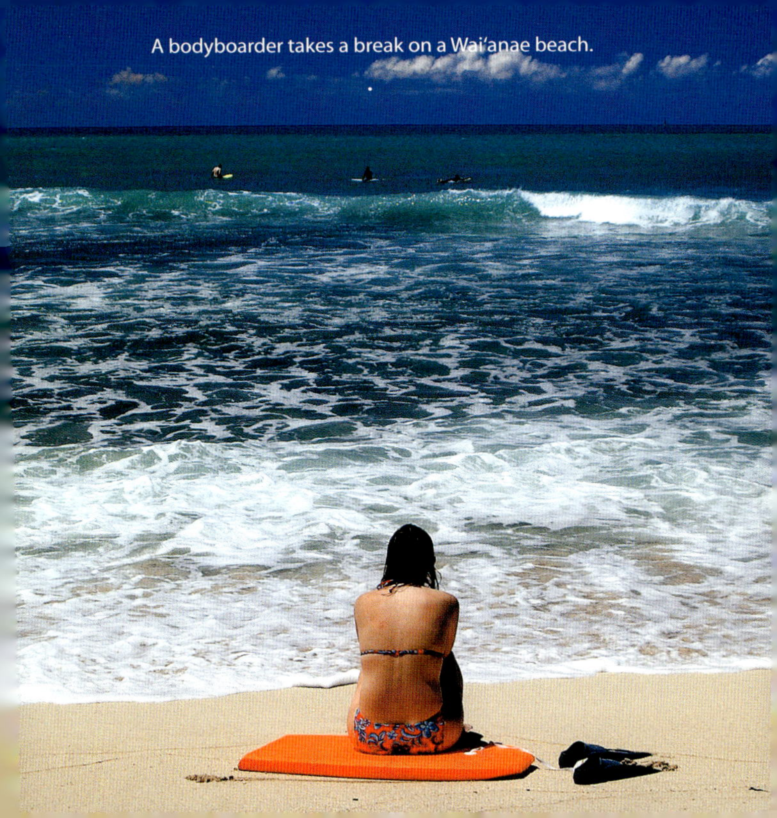

A bodyboarder takes a break on a Waiʻanae beach.

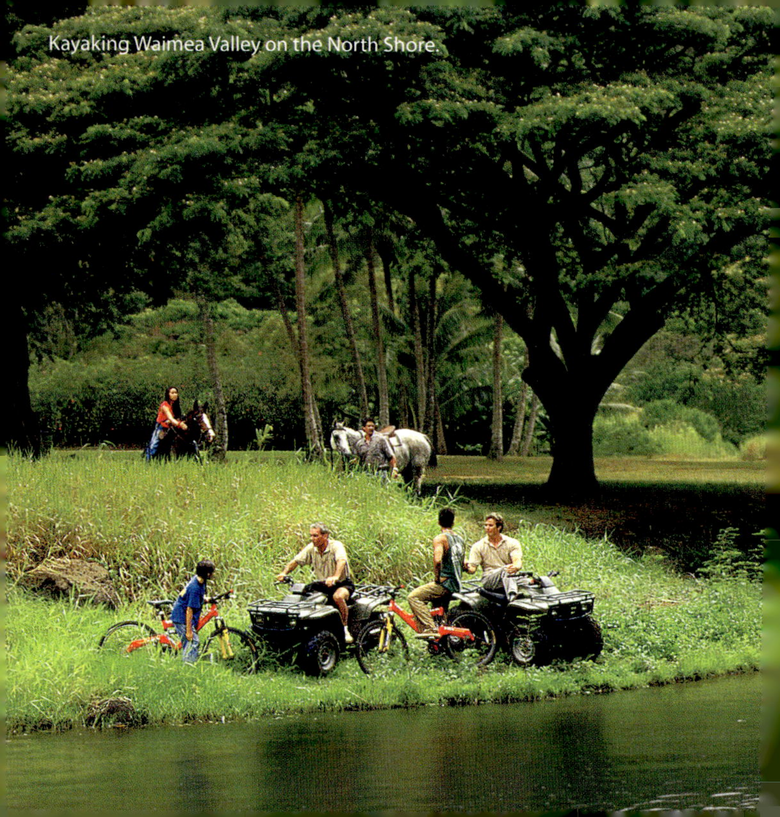

Kayaking Waimea Valley on the North Shore.

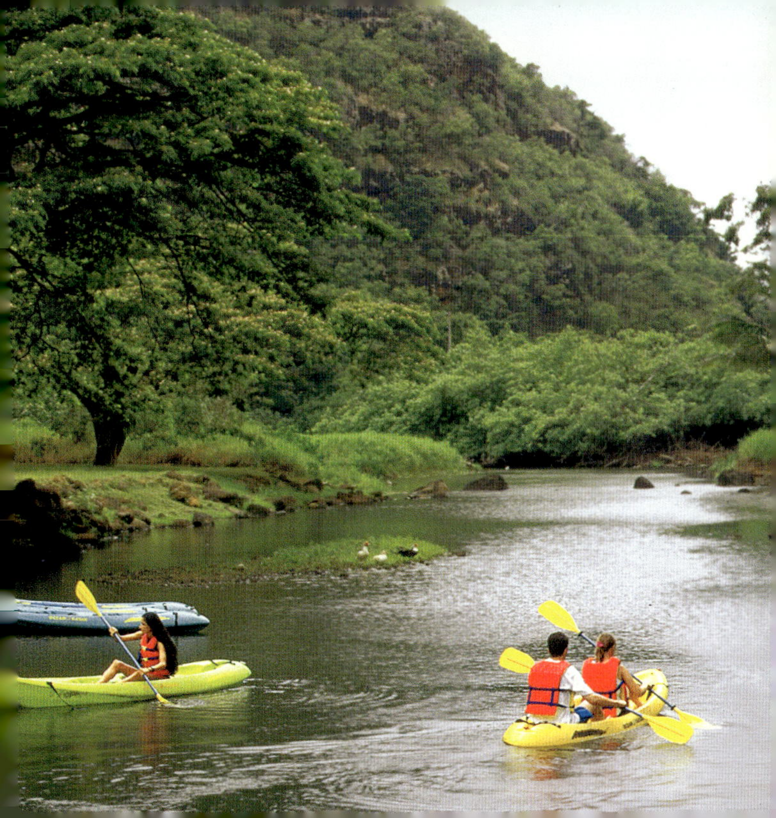

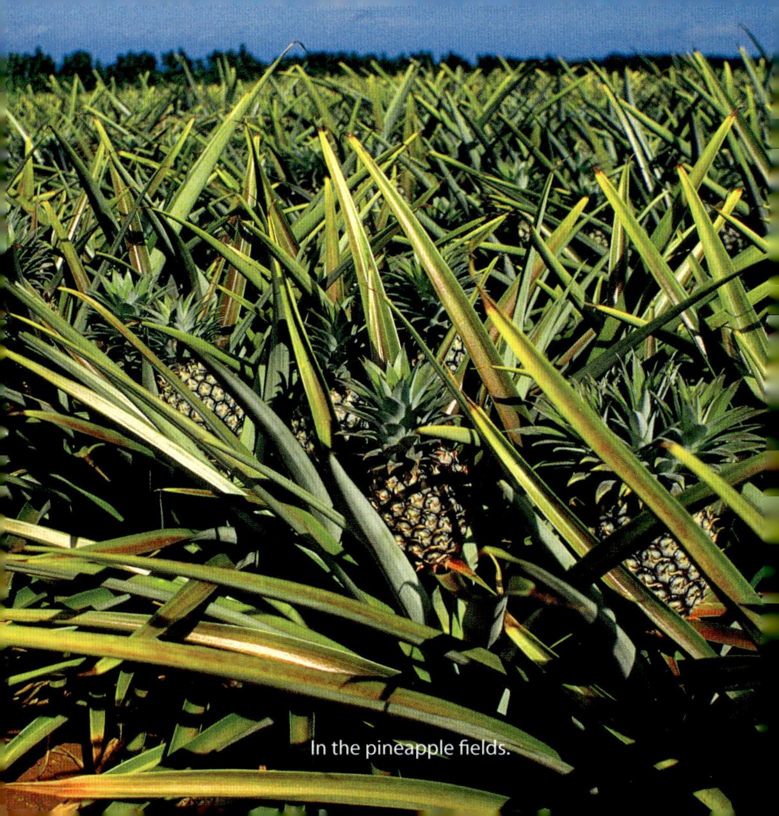

In the pineapple fields.

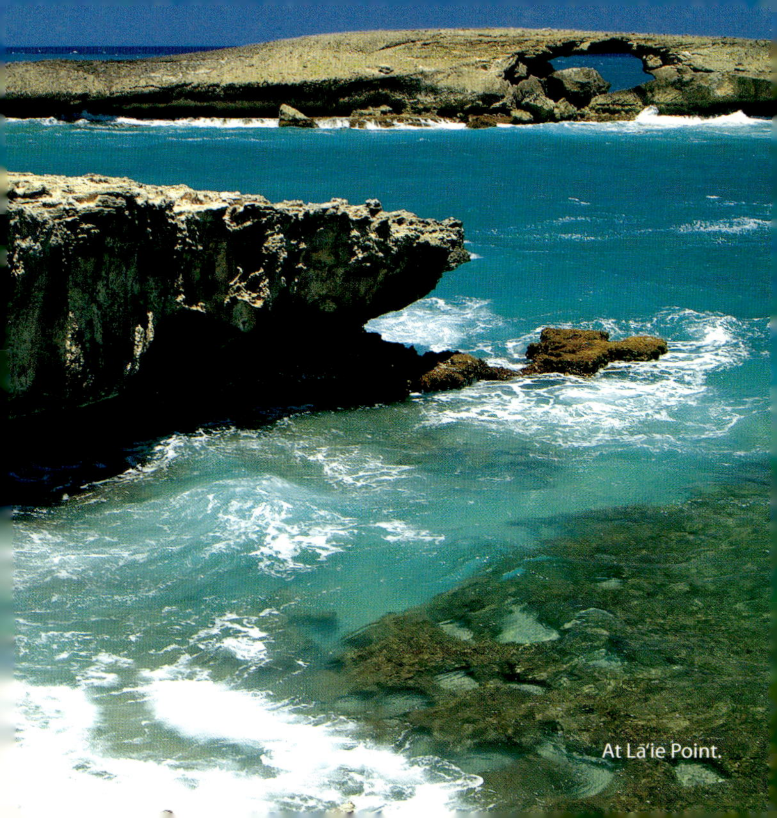

At La'ie Point.

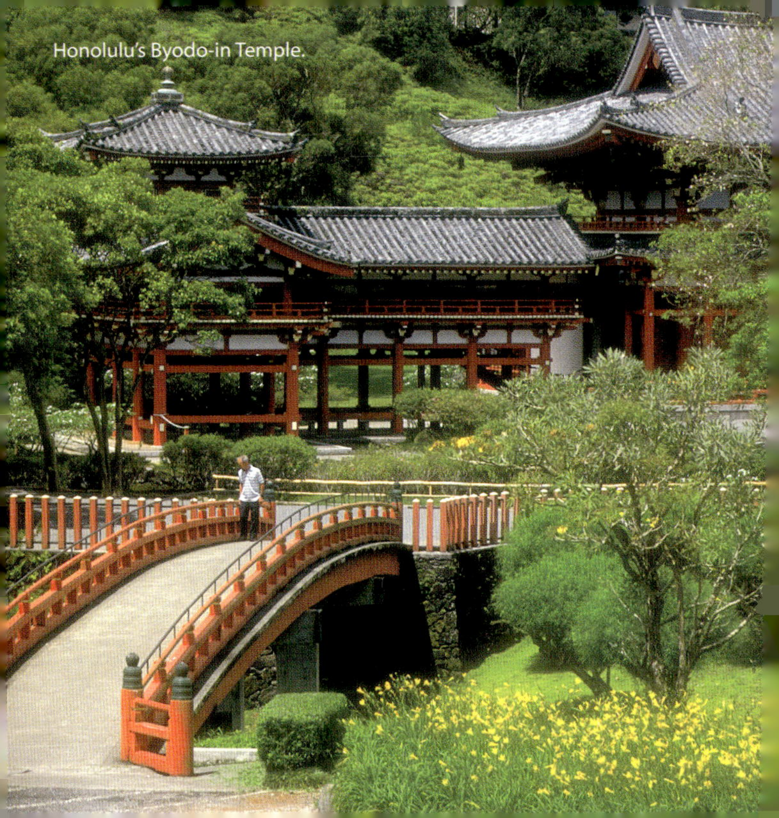

Honolulu's Byodo-in Temple.

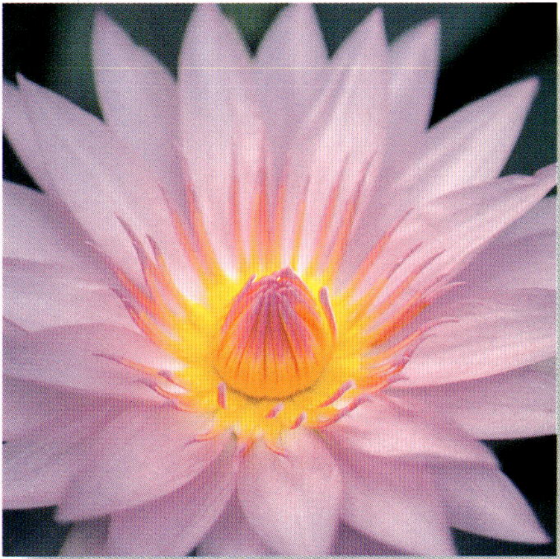

Lotus blossoms grace the ponds surrounding Byodo-In Temple.

Bishop Museum's Hawai'i Hall.

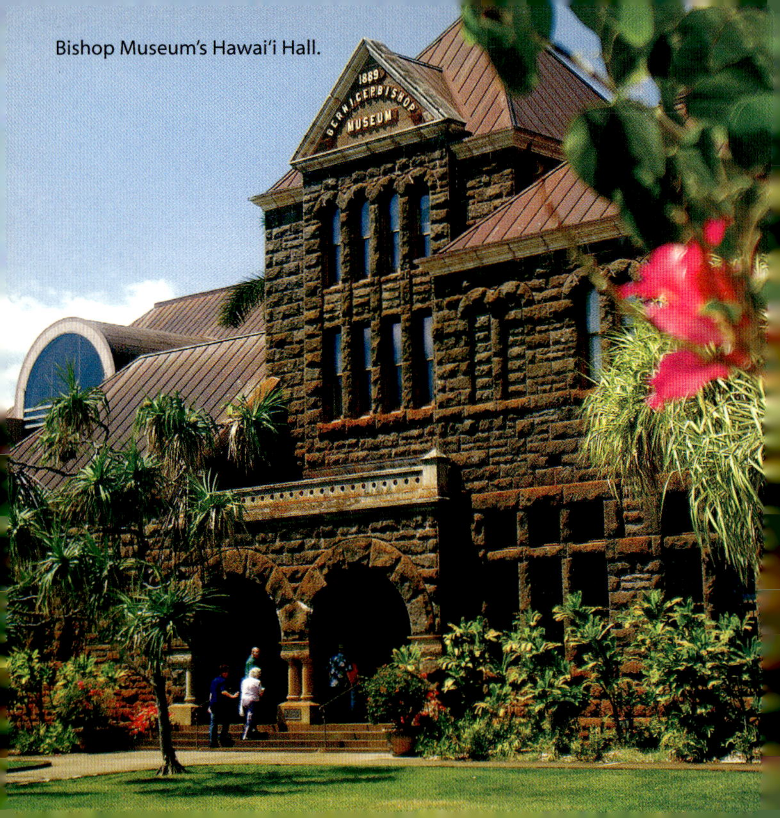

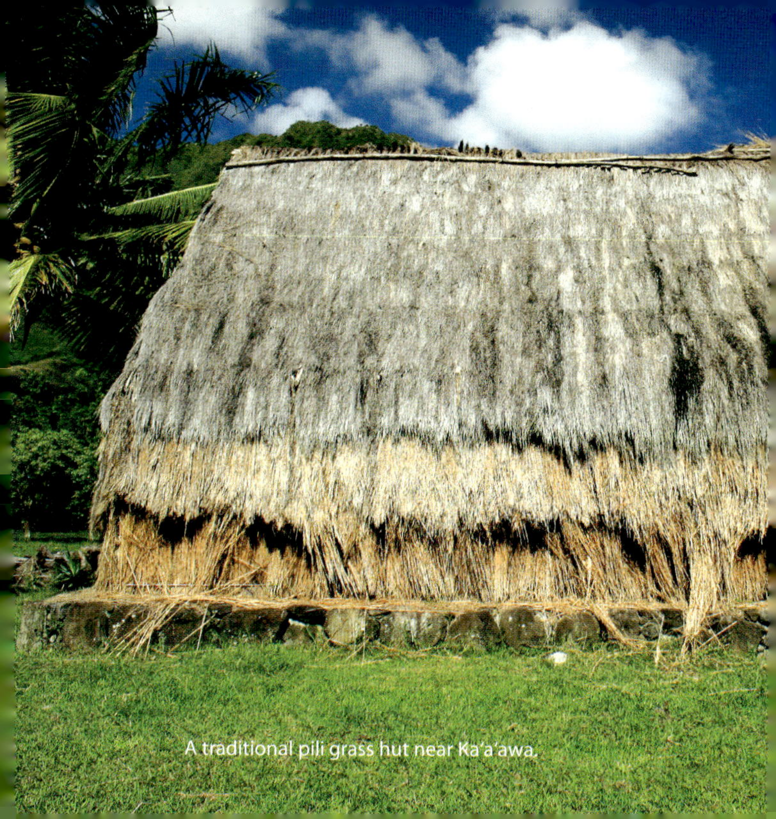

A traditional pili grass hut near Ka'a'awa.

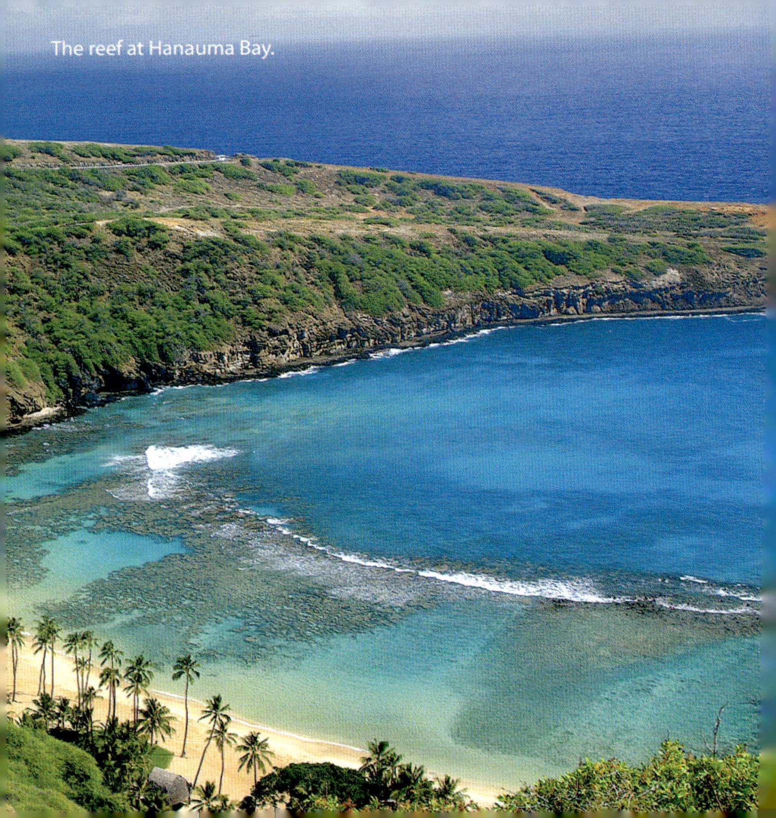

The reef at Hanauma Bay.

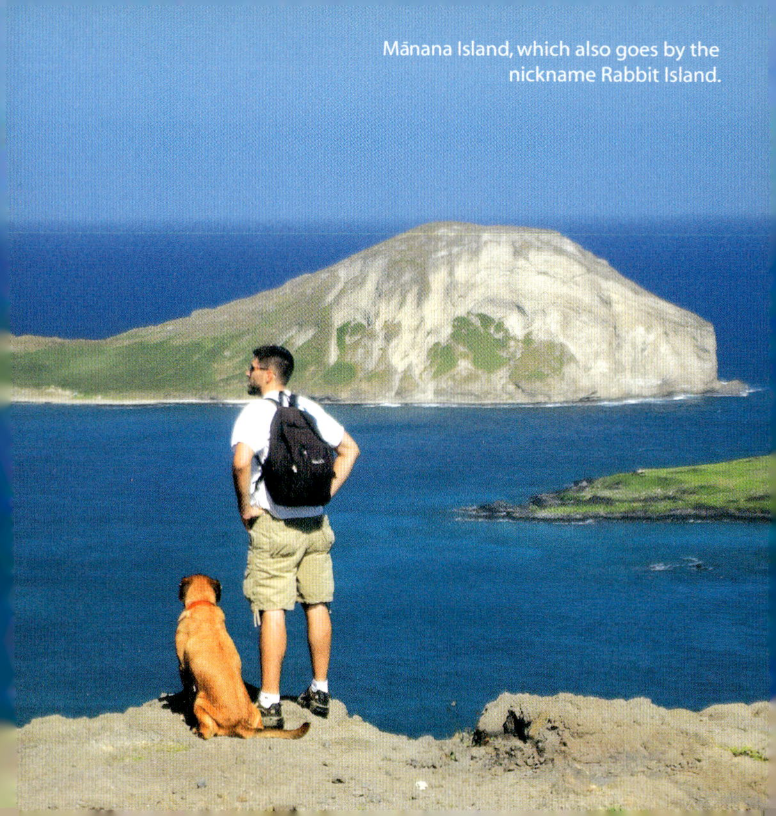

Mānana Island, which also goes by the nickname Rabbit Island.

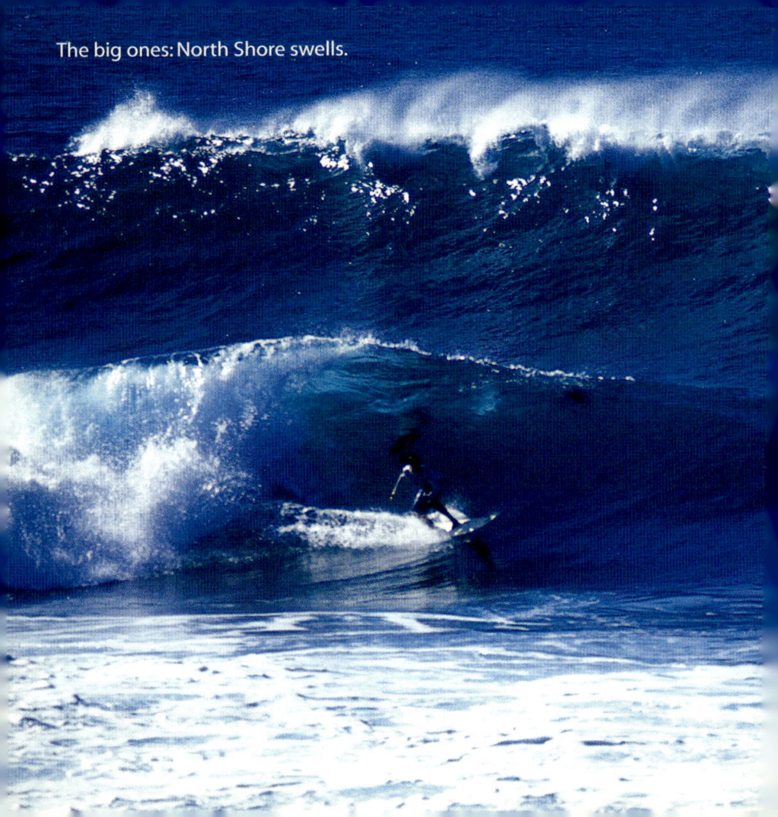

The big ones: North Shore swells.

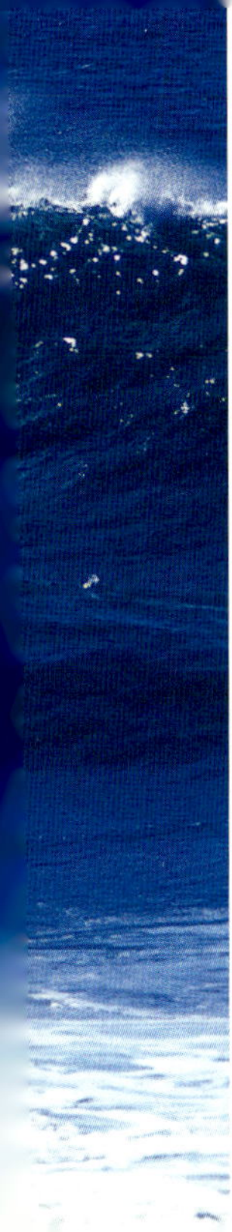

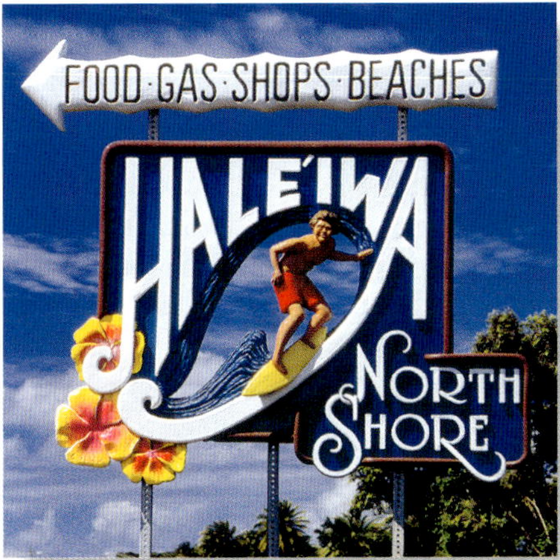

The little surf capital of the world: Hale'iwa.

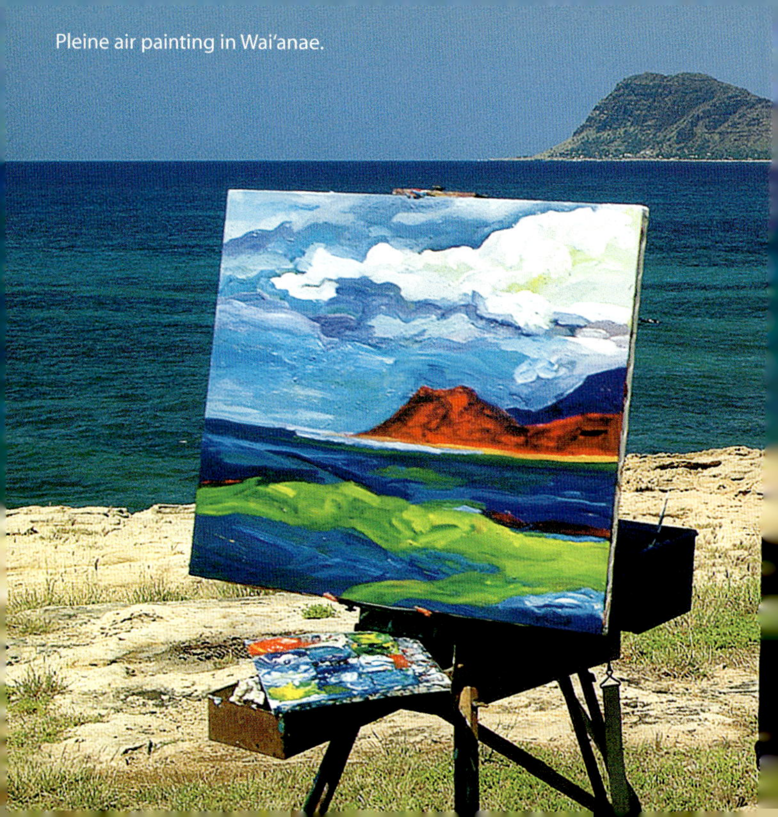

Pleine air painting in Wai‘anae.

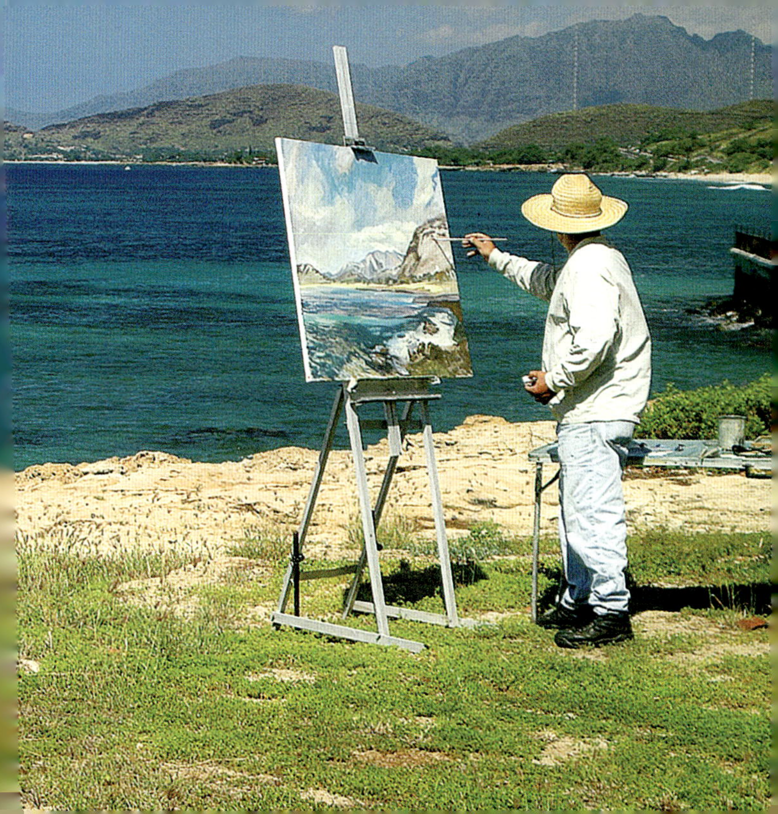

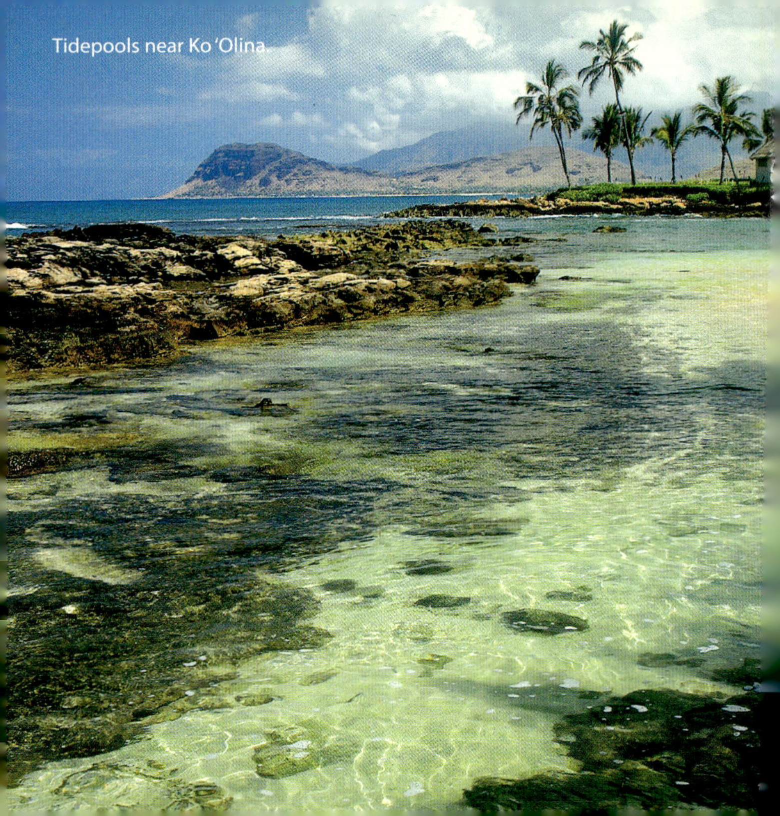
Tidepools near Ko 'Olina.

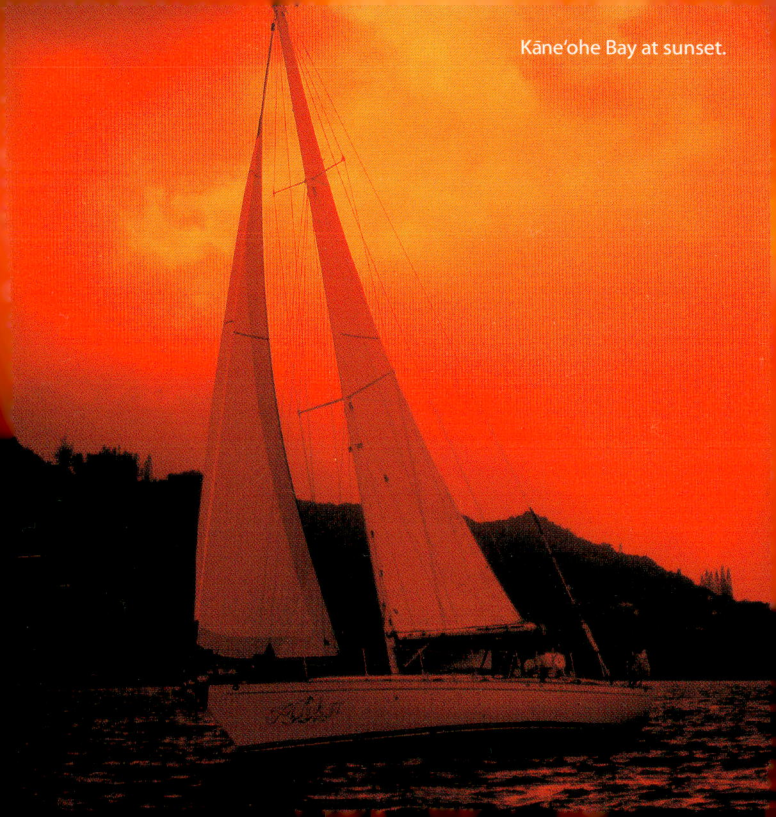

Kāne'ohe Bay at sunset.

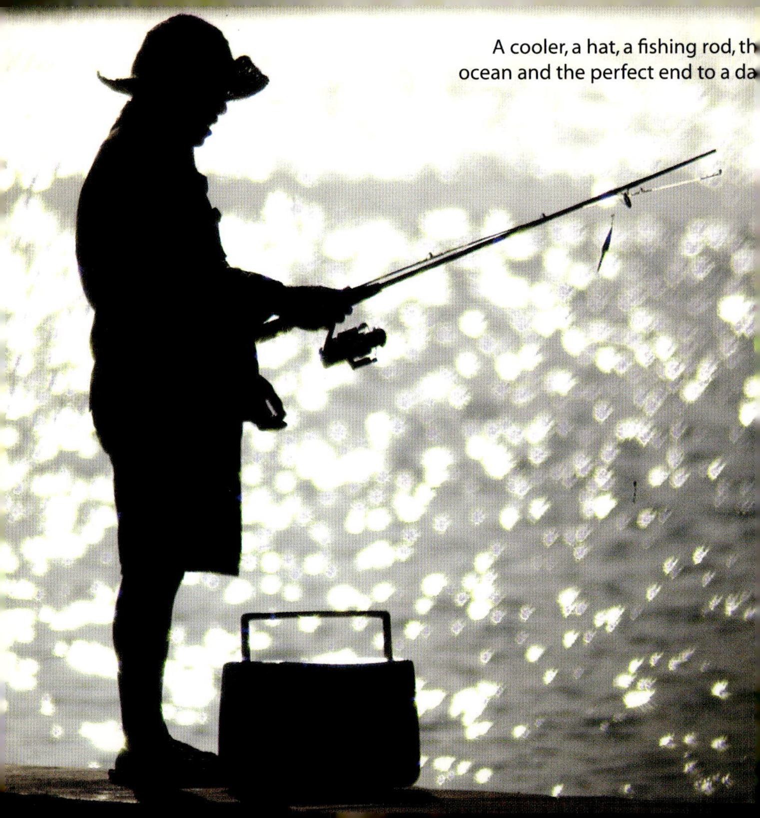

A cooler, a hat, a fishing rod, th
ocean and the perfect end to a da